Don't go around
saying the world owes
you a living.
The world owes you

NOTHING.

It was here first.

~ Mark Twain

✓Start RIGHT ...Stay RIGHT

Every Employee's Straight-Talk Guide to JOB SUCCESS

STEVE VENTURA

A **WALK THE TALK** *Resource*

The  Company

Helping organizations achieve success through Ethical
Leadership and Values-Based Business Practices

To order additional copies of this handbook, or for information on
other WALK THE TALK® products and services,
contact us at
1.888.822.9255
or visit our website at
www.walkthetalk.com

Start RIGHT ... Stay RIGHT

Printed in the United States of America
10 9 8 7 6

Produced by Steve Ventura
Printed by MultiAd

ISBN 1-885228-59-7

9 781885 228598

Congratulations!
You have a job!

Not everyone today can make that claim, and that makes you one of the lucky ones. But while you're fortunate to be working, luck alone won't keep you employed – and it sure as heck won't bring you the future success you need. That's why you've received this handbook ... that's why you've been given this valuable gift.

Whether you're a seasoned coworker or someone just starting employment, no matter if this is your ideal job or merely one stop on a larger career journey, you "oughtta wanna" be successful. *You owe it to your organization* – the one that not only gives you money, but also entrusts you with its resources, its customers, and its future. *You owe it to your coworkers* – those whose welfare, performance, and success are inextricably linked to yours. Most importantly, *you owe it to yourself* – the one who ultimately benefits from, or is hampered by, the track record you add to each day.

There are two areas in which job success is determined:

1. Technical aspects and skills – the "how to's" of compiling reports, programming computers, processing orders, fixing plumbing, serving customers, etc.

2. "The other stuff" – the conduct and attitude-related behaviors you exhibit in the performance of your duties.

Because the second area ("the other stuff") is so critical yet often overlooked in training, I've chosen to make it the topic of this book.

Although there are no guarantees in business (or in life), building a reputation as a top-notch employee increases your odds for:

■ Enjoying job protection and security.

■ Receiving developmental assignments and training.

■ Being considered for promotion ("upward mobility").

■ Landing a similar or better job elsewhere – if the need arises.

All of these offer the paychecks that allow you to do and acquire the things that are important to you and the people you care about.

Now if all this means nothing, you might as well not waste your time reading any further. Give the book to someone who *does* care and will make good use of it. The road sign found on *your* career path likely reads "NOWHERE." Just find yourself a comfortable seat and watch those who *are* interested in success zoom past you. In today's fluctuating economy, there's an ever-increasing number of people who are ready and willing to take advantage of opportunities that others choose to squander.

If, however, you're like most people who want to reap the benefits that come with job success – read on!

The information that follows is for YOU. Pay attention to it ... use it ... SUCCEED WITH IT!

Contents

Take responsibility for yourself

If you were like most teenagers, you couldn't wait to grow up. Betcha you wanted the freedom and privileges that come with adulthood just as fast as you could get them. "Treat me like an adult," "Let me come and go as I please," and "You need to let me make my own decisions" were probably just a few of your rallying cries. Right? Sure! That's natural. But then here's what undoubtedly happened: You grew up (age wise, at least) and found that attached to those freedoms and privileges were a ton of responsibilities. There were *more* rules to follow, not less. Suddenly, the rest of the world was holding YOU accountable for your behavior and decisions (instead of those who raised you) – AND STILL IS.

Here's the straight scoop: Unless someone is holding a gun to your head, everything you do in life is your choice. And that's especially true at work. You *choose* how you conduct yourself; you *choose* how you treat others; you *choose* your "attitude," and how you respond to stress and adversity; you *choose* the levels of honesty and integrity that you display. Ultimately, you *choose* whether to take your personal responsibility seriously or to shirk it like some "deadbeat."

The kicker to remember here is that there are consequences to each choice you (we) make. Bad choices usually have bad ramifications. And blaming others for your poor choices is a waste of time. The "It's someone else's fault!" victim mentality is a sure path to nowhere.

Want to be truly successful? Take responsibility for yourself and your choices. And choose well.

You are what you choose to be!

Contribute to others' success

Imagine this scenario: You're struggling to get your work done. Next to you is a coworker with a little extra time who has the knowledge and skills to help. Do you say to yourself: *He doesn't need to pitch in. It's not his job to help me do mine?* Or, are your inner thoughts more like: *He can see I'm falling behind. You'd think he'd offer to help bail me out!* No doubt, you'd be thinking and feeling the latter – hoping for, and perhaps even expecting, a little help. After all, you're all on the same team ... you're all "in this together" ... helping a co-worker is ultimately serving the customer, and that's what you're there for. Right? Right!

Now reverse the story. *You're* the one with the ability to help, and next to you is a coworker who's struggling. What are you more likely to do? Answer honestly now. Are you more likely to offer help or to look the other way? Hopefully, your first instinct would be to pitch in. And if that's the case, you're a "team player" – one of the key characteristics of a successful employee. Congratulations!

So if you're looking to get noticed, appreciated, and perhaps even pro-moted, look for opportunities to contribute to the success of the people around you. Share your talents and your time to help others learn, grow, and get through tough situations. Just make sure that helping others doesn't prevent you from getting your *own* work done.

By the way, if you happen to be the kind of person who *would* look the other way when someone needs assistance, consider changing your habits. Or at least fasten your seat belt – because what goes around will most definitely come around ... backatcha. And you truly will be de-serving of all the help you *don't* get!

Put customers first

Put *your* customer hat on for a minute and do a little reflection. Have you ever stood in a business, waiting to be served, while the person who's supposed to be waiting on you completes some paperwork, makes a phone call, performs some other duty – or worse yet, chats with a coworker? If you have, you know how frustrating it can be. That employee is putting his or her business before yours. The wrong person is doing the waiting. And saying "I'll be with you in a minute" doesn't cut it.

That's just one of many examples of business people failing to realize that customers are supposed to come first. And if you intend to be successful at work, you'd better not fall in that same trap.

Maybe you're thinking: *This doesn't apply to me ... I don't deal directly with our customers.* Well think again! Fact is, EVERYONE has customers – whether they be members of the general public who patronize your business or other employees within your organization for whom you provide services. Your job exists because those customers exist. Fail to serve them properly – put your needs before theirs – and they just might take their business elsewhere. And then elsewhere is probably where you'll be working. Not good!

Remember: The only reason a customer should wait for you to serve them is because you're serving another customer. Even then, they shouldn't have to wait too long.

Words to Remember

For true success ask yourself these four questions:
Why? Why not? Why not me? Why not now?
~James Allen

The only thing that separates successful people from the
ones who aren't is the willingness to work very, very hard.
~Helen Gurley Brown

Success is a journey not a destination. The doing is usually more
important than the outcome. Not everyone can be number one.
~Arthur Ashe

The elevator to success is out of order. You'll have to use
the stairs ... one step at a time.
~Joe Girard

The only place you find success before work is in the dictionary.
~May V. Smith

Success is the sum of small efforts, repeated day in
and day out.
~Robert Collier

The road to success is lined with many tempting parking spaces.
~Source Unknown

Be a "team player"

So I was watching my favorite pro sports franchise lose a must-win game on television last night. They're out ... they're history ... the season is over. "How in the world can that happen," I ask myself, "with all the talent we have?" Then, the coach answers my question in a post-game interview: "We're loaded with superstars, but today, we just didn't work together ... as a team." What a loss – what a lesson.

Business, like many of the games in athletics, is a team "sport." You have a collection of individuals who must work together to accomplish a common goal. While the players contribute in varying degrees, no one person can produce a victory on his or her own. Each member of the team has a role – a position. And each position has a variety of responsibilities: sometimes you shoot, sometimes you assist, some-times you block ... sometimes you're in the spotlight, sometimes you're in the trenches. And two things are for sure: 1) Everyone on the team ends up being an equal winner or an equal loser, and 2) Limelight-grabbing ball hogs don't last very long.

Are you a team player at work? Do you give your best effort regardless of the role you play? Are you willing to do the things that are needed to help the group succeed? Do you work at being cooperative and com-municating well with your coworkers? Are you considerate of others? Do you accept and value others' ideas – especially when those ideas are different from yours? Can you be counted on to carry your share of the load?

If your answers to the above questions are all "yes," success is defi-nitely in your future. More interested in only being the star? Just re-member that even *they* get traded when teams lose!

Volunteer ... and show some initiative

Yep, here they are ... you probably knew they were coming – the "V" and "I" words: Volunteer and Initiative. They're two more factors leading to job success – and concepts that many people avoid like the plague.

The rap on both is that they can lead to more work. Well, DUH! Yeah! Of course they represent more work. So what? Extra effort is what increases your ability to make a difference ... to develop, grow, and show what you can do. That's how you separate yourself from the rest of the pack. That's precisely why volunteering and displaying initiative *are* success factors.

Put yourself in a boss's shoes for a minute. Who are you more likely to identify (and treat) as a rising star – an employee who just does what he or she is supposed to, or one who is always looking for additional ways to contribute? *There's* a no-brainer! Of course it's the person who seeks additional responsibility ... the person who *finds* things to do rather than waiting for those things to find him or her.

Fact is, to be noticed, you have to do things that will *get* you noticed. Remember that the next time you see something that needs to be done; remember that the next chance you have to volunteer for a special duty or project. Raise your hand, step forward, and say: "I'd like a shot at that." From going out of your way to pick up a piece of trash, to offering to stay late to help fill a customer's request – just DO IT!

Wanna be successful at work? Eliminate "It's not *my* job" from your thoughts ... and your vocabulary.

Follow the rules

Getting tired of following rules? Think there are way too many restrictions to remember and abide by? Well try imagining a world *without* rules. Picture driving your car without signals, signs, lane markers, or traffic regulations … or playing a sport with no time limits, no defined playing areas, and no fouls. Now, picture those same scenarios *with* rules – but each driver or player gets to pick and choose the ones he or she will follow and those that will be ignored. In both cases you'd end up with total CHAOS, not to mention unfair and dangerous conditions for the participants. Nope, rules aren't bad; they're good. We need them … we rely on them – in our private lives and at work. They provide stability and guidance. And they allow each of us to compete on a "level playing field."

Most of the rules in your workplace represent nothing more than common sense and therefore may seem unnecessary. But, unfortunately, common sense isn't as common as we'd like to think. Too often, some yahoo, somewhere, does something stupid – forcing the organization to establish yet another written regulation for everyone to follow. That's okay, however, because rules help us stay on track and avoid dumb and counterproductive actions ourselves.

Successful people accept and understand three key concepts:

1. Rules typically exist for good reasons.

2. Employees are responsible for knowing and abiding by ALL of those rules.

3. If you think a rule is stupid or problematic, you try to get it changed but you never ignore it.

Avoid penalties. Win the game. Play by the rules.

Safe Assumptions

Most people realize that making assumptions is bad and can get you into some serious trouble. As the saying goes: "When you ASSUME, you make an ASS of U and ME." Nevertheless, as humans we all tend to make them. So here are some safe ones … things you can feel okay in assuming:

- The e-mails you send will be seen by more people than those they're addressed to.

- Things said "just between you and me" won't stay that way.

- The time you pick to take a long break or lunch will be the same time your boss looks for you.

- The "minor" rule you choose to ignore will be the pet peeve of the manager that catches you.

- Call in sick so you can do something else and you will be seen by someone who knows you should be working.

- Treat one customer poorly, and ten people will hear about it – including someone who has authority over you.

- Your ability to get "another job" will be directly related to how well you do on the job you have now.

- Whenever you think "no one will know," someone will.

- Whenever you think "no one will care," someone will.

- Whenever you think "it will never be missed," it will.

- Whenever you think you're as good as you need to be, you aren't.

Work the hours you're paid for

Come in ten minutes before my starting time to get ready to work? Don't be ridiculous! "Shut down" ten minutes before my shift ends to get ready to leave? Hey, that's perfectly okay!

Sound familiar? Probably! There are more than a few people who share those thoughts. You might even have "a friend" whose mind works that way. What's up with that? I don't get it. Actually, I *do* get it ... I just don't agree with it. And if your friend wants to be successful, he or she needs to do some rethinking.

Most organizations have the expectation that employees will begin working at their start time – and continue working (minus breaks) until the end of their scheduled hours. What a novel idea! If you really think about it, expecting people to actually work the hours they're being paid for is very reasonable and very fair. It's just like paying your auto mechanic for an hour's worth of labor: You expect your car to get the full hour of work, right? Sure. But look around ... and maybe even examine your own occasional behavior. You'll find it doesn't always work that way.

Check out the "stragglers" – the people who wander in as the clock strikes their appointed hour. By the time they put their stuff away, fire-up their equipment, hit the rest room, and grab a cup of coffee, ten minutes are shot. (That's compounded when they slide in a few minutes late.) And then, of course, there's the end of the day when many engage in the all-too-common practice of "preparing to leave" (i.e., shutting down ten or more minutes early in order to walk out the door precisely at the end of one's workday).

In both of the previous examples, employers are losing productive time that they're paying for ... they're being shorted.

Now I've known a few people in my working lifetime who wouldn't think twice about ripping off "the company" for ten minutes here, fifteen minutes there. Ironically, those are the very same people who would pitch the biggest fit if ever shorted on their paychecks. Interesting, isn't it? By the way, that's called "hypocrisy"!

Imagine you have your own business and that you have two employees. One of them is productively working throughout her shift. The other regularly does his preparation (to start and to leave) on *your* time. Who will *you* rely on? Who are *you* going to train and promote? Who are *you* going to help be successful. I sure as heck know who it is for me!

So here's the deal: If you want to be successful, make sure you work – really (and productively) work – the hours you're being paid for. Be willing to throw in a few extra minutes when needed, and you'll stand out even more. It's that simple ... it's that easy.

Note ...

Obviously, the message of this section is directed primarily to hourly employees. If you're a *salaried* employee who typically works long days, you may be thinking: "I'd love to JUST work the hours I'm paid for!" Trust me, I can relate.

It's not unusual for people like us to watch others walk out the door knowing *we* still have a lot remaining to accomplish before calling it a day ... or a weekend. Those of us who share that boat have to accept that it's a fact of business life that comes with the job. We need to make the best use of the hours we work – no matter how many and how long they may be.

Fact is, long hours don't always equate to productive hours. And it just may be that learning to work more productively can reduce the total time you need to put in – and increase your personal success at the same time.

Exceed expectations

If I were limited to passing along only two guidelines for job success, there's no question in my mind that they would be:

1. **Know what's expected of you.**
2. **Exceed those expectations.**

I've known many successful people in my life, and none of them got that way by just doing what was expected or required. They all separated themselves from the rest of the pack by doing more, and by doing better, than what they were "supposed to do." *You* can as well.

Start by making sure you have a handle on how your boss, your organization, and your customers expect you to perform. How can you find out? Try reviewing your job description (if one exists), asking your manager, reflecting on your last performance review, requesting clarification at the start of a new project, probing a client, or "picking the brain" of a successful and respected coworker who has a similar job.

Once you've identified how (and how well) you're supposed to do things, raise the bar on yourself. If you're supposed to produce twenty widgets per hour, shoot for twenty-two; if you're expected to make ten service calls each day, go for eleven; if you're expected to keep your work area clean, keep it spotless; if an assignment is due on Thursday, get it in on Wednesday; if you're expected to make sure customers are satisfied, try to make them ecstatic.

Look for every opportunity to go the extra mile. That's how you become extra special ... and extra successful.

Keep your commitments

Trustworthy. Dependable. Reliable. Do those words describe you? Would others say that your word is your bond? The answer to each of those questions needs to be a resounding "yes" for success to be in your future (and your present).

Most successful people place a premium on keeping their promises and commitments. If they say they'll do something – whether "important" or seemingly insignificant – they remember it ... and they DO it. They count on the fact that people can count on *them*. And they understand that statements like "I was gonna," "I meant to," and "I haven't forgotten" all translate the same way: I JUST DIDN'T DO IT! Those are excuses. They're close to meaningless. They're ersatz (look it up).

With the exception of the few unethical jerks out there, all people really do *intend* to keep "their word" and their promises. But good intentions alone won't take you very far. You get no "points" for them. Points come only when you deliver.

So, don't make promises lightly; don't make ones you can't (or really don't intend) to keep. And when you *do* make commitments to your boss, to customers, or to coworkers, do whatever it takes to make good on them. Those people are expecting you to keep your word. Your reputation is at stake ... your success is on the line.

Get with change

You no sooner learn and get comfortable with your job and boom, "they" change it. You've almost completed a project and wham, "they" decide to go back to the drawing board. You schedule your time to meet a deadline and whack, "they" move it up. Sound familiar? Either you already have, or eventually will, come face-to-face with change and the frustrations that often accompany it. It's inevitable – for all of us. And if you're looking to enhance your job success, the best advice I can offer is: GET OVER IT ... ACCEPT IT ... DEAL WITH IT ... and even APPRECIATE IT!

When it comes to the old adage, "The only constant is change," truer words were never spoken – especially in the business arena. Organizations, today, operate at warp speed. To survive and prosper, they must respond quickly to changing conditions. Business people who lack flexibility place themselves in harm's way. Don't be one of them!

So how do you learn to deal with change effectively ... and sanely? By continually reminding yourself that:

- Although the timing may stink, there's usually a good reason behind the changes you and others are required to make.

- Those requiring or dictating change (typically managers) rarely control the circumstances they must respond to ... and if they *don't* respond, you lose.

- Change helps you battle your competition and poor economic conditions. No change equals no progress.

- Everything you now enjoy was a "change" at one time.

- The fact that you must make changes means you're still employed.

- Your job is to do whatever the organization needs done. If that involves change, **so be it!**

Success-Killing Phrases
(and thoughts)
TO AVOID

It's not MY job!

It's not my problem!

Everyone else does it!

That will never work!

We tried that before!

We've always done it that way!

It doesn't matter!

It's good enough!

Some rules were meant to be broken!

Someone else will do it!

I don't care what other people think!

I could get more done if it wasn't for all these customers!

I don't need any help!

I know everything I need to know!

Rumor has it that ...!

Did you hear the joke about the (racial/sexual term) ...?

I don't care!

I just do what I'm told!

I can always find another job!

I just put in my time and then get outta here!

They don't pay me enough to do that!

Be considerate of others

Don't know about you, but I've got a real problem with inconsiderate people. You know them – they're the ones who behave like the workplace is an extension of their homes. These are the people who leave messes for others to clean up (or live with), play the music *they* like (which some others hate) way too loud, hog equipment as if no one else's work matters, expect others to immediately respond to their every need ... and exhibit a bunch more selfish and inconsiderate behaviors.

See, here's the deal: The workplace is a *shared* environment. That means everyone has the same rights as everyone else – including NOT having to accept or endure the personal preferences (or disturbing behaviors) of others ... and yours.

You're not the only person in the world, so don't act like it. Instead, enhance your success at work by building a reputation for being a thoughtful, considerate coworker. How? By doing things like:

- Cleaning up after yourself.

- Sharing – not monopolizing – equipment and resources.

- Filling the copy machine with paper for the next person – even though there were a few sheets left when you finished.

- Restocking (or letting the appropriate person know) when you take the last of the supplies.

- Keeping your music and your voice down.

- Respecting others' time by not interrupting them – and not expecting them to serve your every need "on the spot."

- Immediately stopping behaviors that coworkers tell you are disturbing.

Don't "whine" or spread negativity

The scene here is all too commonplace: A boss or coworker "wrongs" you – or merely does something you don't like – and before your day ends, *everyone* you know has heard about it (from you). Everyone, that is, except the person you have the problem with.

Does the shoe fit? Of course it does! Each of us, at one time or another, has spread a tale of woe to our own little circle of "poor you" supporters or fellow behind-the-back gossipers. It happens all the time: chatter around the proverbial water cooler; whispers in cubicles; e-mails to a certain few.

People raggin' on people. I'm pretty sure it's not genetic. Last time I checked, no one yet had been born with a **W**-gene (as in **W**hine) or a **G**-gene (as in **G**ossip) that made such behaviors inherent and unconscious. So why do we do it? Maybe it's because misery really does love company (a.k.a. "I somehow feel better when I'm able to suck other people into my funk."). Maybe we're just looking for sympathy, or we're trying to build ourselves up by cutting others down. Maybe it's a way of hurting the other person. Or perhaps we're just looking for confirmation that he or she is as big a jerk as we think they are.

Why do we do it? IT DOESN'T MATTER! What *does* matter is that talking about others behind their backs is a petty, negative, and counterproductive behavior that degrades them and you ... and accomplishes nothing beyond that!

Got a problem with someone? Talk with *him or her!* State your concern in a respectful manner, and ask for the other person's cooperation in correcting whatever it is that's bugging you.

Give, and earn, respect

Everyone wants it, everyone needs it, but not everyone gets or gives it. The "it" is RESPECT ... and it's something we all need to ratchet up in varying degrees.

There are two types of respect. First is basic human respect – the kind you're entitled to merely by being born. Everyone deserves it equally because through birth, everyone *is* equal – we're all living, breathing human beings.

This type of respect is based on the fact that other people's needs, hopes, rights, dreams, ideas, and inherent worth are just as important and valuable as your own. And it's demonstrated through specific behaviors such as:

- Treating everyone with dignity, courtesy, and equality.

- Appreciating "different" backgrounds, cultures, and ideas – not expecting everyone to be just like you ... unless you're perfect (yeah, right).

- Avoiding ethnic and sexually-oriented references and "humor" (which, by the way, *isn't* all that humorous but *is* very illegal).

- Talking *with* people – not *at* them ... and not *about* them.

This first kind of respect is purely and simply an entitlement (a right) – one that comes with our human skin ... regardless of its color or condition. We all deserve it.

The second type of respect is the kind you EARN by your actions. This kind is different from the first, because it's based on *who* you are (the quality of your character) rather than *what* you are (a human being); it comes from behavior rather than mere birth. And since not everyone exhibits the same behavior and character, not everyone gets the same amount of this respect.

Want your judgement, opinions, and skills respected? Well, ya gotta earn that by demonstrating judgement, opinions, and skills that are respect-*worthy*. Want to be respected for dependability? Ya gotta earn that, too — by consistently BEING dependable. Feel it's important to be trusted? Yep, you guessed it — trust must be earned in order to be deserved. Finally, for leaders at all levels: Need the respect of your people in order to lead effectively? The response is the same — you must EARN it ... by being a person of integrity!

If you're looking to hold a prominent place in the ranks of the truly successful, you must devote constant effort and attention to:

- Treating everyone with the dignity he or she deserves as a human being.

- EARNing the additional respect of character you need in order to succeed.

As the song goes: "R. E. S. P. E. C. T. Find out what it means to me."

Recognize the inherent worth of all human beings.

Eliminate derogatory words and phrases from your vocabulary.

Speak with people – not at them ... or about them.

Practice empathy. Walk awhile in others' shoes.

Earn the respect of your coworkers through your behaviors.

Consider others' feelings before speaking and acting.

Treat everyone with dignity and courtesy.

---

*I'm not concerned with your liking or disliking me ...
all I ask is that you respect me as a human being.*
~Jackie Robinson

Embrace diversity

Ever find yourself thinking that people who are different from you (different skin color, religion, ethnic background, culture, way of speaking, etc.) are strange, wrong, or perhaps something worse (and derogatory)? If so, it's time to unscrew the top of your head, throw out some of the garbage in there, and catch up with the human race.

No two people are exactly the same. So, if being different were to equal being wrong, *everyone* would be wrong – including YOU! That would definitely be bad. But you know what would be worse? If everyone were exactly alike! In that case, we'd all look, sound, and act the same. We'd only need one type of food, one way of thinking, one sport, one kind of music, one type (and color) of car, one style of clothes, one political party – simply one of everything. With everyone the same, we wouldn't have creative "oddballs" inventing new technologies and creature comforts to improve our lives; we wouldn't have "foreigners" buying our products and services; we wouldn't have the blending of cultures and ideas that afford us new and enriching experiences. Most importantly, if everyone and everything were the same, we wouldn't have *choices*.

Sometimes being different IS being wrong. And in those cases, we have laws, rules, and procedures to control inappropriate behavior. Most of the time, however, different isn't wrong – it's just different. And that's a fact that everyone needs to accept. Better yet, that's a fact that everyone needs to *embrace*. It is, after all, what allows *you* to be different from someone else ... and to be proud of it!

So, work on maximizing your respect for diversity. Appreciate individuals who are "different" – especially those of other races, cultures, creeds, and national origins. In this land, unless you happen to be Native American, your ancestors WERE those different people ... and you're still one of them.

Keep learning

Looking for a fast way to bring your job success and your career to a screeching halt? Adopt the mind set that you already know everything you *need* to know at work. That'll do it for sure!

There are a lot of people out there who figure that once they've completed orientation training and been around for a while, they're set. Just do the work each day and go home. Well, that kind of thinking probably will keep you employed, but it sure isn't gonna take you anywhere. And if that's where *your* head is at, get ready to watch people who have a thirst for knowledge, learning, and personal development zoom right past you.

Look around. You don't have to be a brain surgeon to figure it out. Things are changing everywhere in business. There are new products, new processes, and new technologies at every turn. And in most cases, knowledge becomes obsolete before you have a chance to fully use it. Either you keep up, or you get left in the dust of those who do. It's that simple.

So, if a successful career is the target in your sights, become an ongoing learning machine. Request additional training; learn more about your products and services; read job and industry-related publications; keep up with what's happening in other parts of your organization; "pick the brains" of knowledgeable coworkers; take a business course at your local community college; and (this one is critical) willingly accept new duties and responsibilities that will help you develop and grow.

Here's one you can take to the bank:

Those on the *go* are those in the *know*!

Ask for feedback

Two of the most important keys to job success are: 1) Keep doing the things you do well (your strengths), and 2) Correct the things you don't do so well (your weaknesses – a.k.a. "developmental opportunities"). And in order to do both of those, you need to know exactly what your strengths and weaknesses are. To be sure, you'll want to periodically do a self-assessment on where you stand. But the best and most accurate information on your performance must come from others – from your boss, your coworkers, and your customers.

If you happen to work in an organization where feedback is frequently provided to you, great! You're fortunate. Pay attention to what you hear and ACT on the information. If you're like most folks, however, you'll need more performance evaluation data than is given to you. That means you'll have to ASK for it.

Make a habit of posing the *How am I doing?* question to someone at least once a month. Solicit information from your manager, a trusted coworker, or a customer you're serving. To pinpoint specific areas to work on, try asking:

> "What one or two things can I do to be more successful?"
> "What can I do to serve you better in the future?"

You'll be amazed at how many people will be more than willing to tell you what you *need* to hear. And when they do, be sure to thank them. They truly will have given you a gift.

Think asking for feedback is lame? Not all that interested in how you can do a better job? Then don't ask for others' help. Hey, it's your call. Just realize that you'll be at a disadvantage of your own choosing. And those people that *are* willing to ask for – and act on – feedback will appreciate the fact that there's one less person competing with them for success!

Be patient

ere are a few workplace realities you're likely to experience at one time or another:

Not everyone you serve will be as smart as you.

Not everyone you serve will know what they really want or need.

Not everyone you work with will be as talented or as quick as you.

Not everyone you work with will communicate as well as you.

Not everyone you work for will understand what you have to go through.

Some of your coworkers will be smarter, quicker, more talented, and better communicators than you.

And the list goes on!

So how do you deal with these facts of business life? You do it by cutting others – and yourself – a little slack; you do it by being patient ... and avoiding responsive behaviors that make people (including yourself) feel bad, inadequate, or just plain stupid.

If you want people to give you the benefit of the doubt – if you want them to assume that you're doing the best you can – then you've got to make the same assumptions about others as well.

Does that mean you shouldn't help others do better or that you don't need to work on improving your own deficiencies? Of course not! But in the process of doing those, be as understanding as you can.

It's true! Patience IS a virtue! And we *all* could stand to be a little more virtuous.

Be appreciative

Successful people tend to be *grateful* people. They focus on what they *have* rather than what they *don't have*. They look for, and show appreciation for, the positives (people, opportunities, circumstances, etc.) that are all around them – especially at work.

What should you be grateful for ... and how should you show it? Here are a few ideas to get you started:

1. **Appreciate the fact that you have a job** ... and show it by doing the best that you can – and by letting others (including the boss) know that you're happy to be a member of the team.

2. **Appreciate all developmental opportunities** (training, coaching, special assignments, etc.) **you receive** ... and show it by saying "thank you" – and by making the most of the experiences you're given.

3. **Appreciate the efforts and contributions of your coworkers** ... and show it through public and private recognition – and by saying things like: "thanks for making us all look good."

4. **Appreciate the customers who give you their business** ... and show it by giving the best service possible – and by sincerely thanking them for choosing *you* to meet their needs.

Think this is some "touchy-feely" form of organizational propaganda? Think being appreciative is hokey or uncool? Think again! Take stock of the "good stuff" that you have – and that you experience – and be thankful for it. You'll wind up feeling better about yourself ... and others will feel better about you, too.

Think "safety"

There's a handful of things in business that are universally UNcompromisable. Tops on that list is safety. You can't possibly be a success at work unless you're *totally* committed to safe work practices.

Unintentional safety violators are usually good yet careless people who put themselves, their coworkers, and their organizations at unnecessary risk. Intentional, habitual safety violators are much worse. They're dangerous criminals who expose themselves and others to serious – even deadly – consequences. And they have no place in the work environment. Period.

When you examine them, you find that most safety rules and regulations are about common sense standards and behaviors. But because common sense isn't a common characteristic, people sometimes do dumb things. That's why written rules exist; that's why it's critical that you know what those rules *are* ... and that you follow them to the letter.

Safety rules and health standards exist to protect YOU. That's why violating them is stupidity at its greatest. It's like seat belt laws for cars. The belts are there to save *your* life, yet some people refuse to wear them. How dumb is that? It makes no sense at all. But then, safety violations, in general, make no sense at all.

So, when it comes to safety: know the rules ... follow the rules ... use your head ... don't take risks or cut corners ... protect yourself, your coworkers, and your customers.

Practice safe success!

More Words to Remember

Success is more attitude than aptitude.
~Source Unknown

There are no secrets to success. It is the result of preparation, hard work, and learning from failure.
~Colin Powell

Success is nothing more than a few simple disciplines, practiced every day.
~Jim Rohn

The Lord gave us two ends – one to sit on and one to think with. Success depends on which one we use the most.
~Ann Landers

Most of the successful people I've known are the ones who do more listening than talking.
~Bernard M. Baruch

Success doesn't come to you – you go to it.
~Marva Collins

I can't imagine a person becoming a success who doesn't give this game of life everything he's got.
~Walter Cronkite

Think "health"

Expecting some self-help type lecture on getting and staying healthy? Forget it! This isn't about preachy lectures … it's about facts. And the facts are that healthy people typically are vibrant, have more energy and drive, display greater focus, experience less stress, and lose fewer days due to illness. The overriding fact: Health is a competitive advantage. It's yet another key to job (and personal) success.

Look around. Who are the most successful people you know? How would you describe their physical conditions? Chances are they're healthy people … they take care of themselves. And that's not a coincidence. Will you be able to find exceptions to that if you look hard enough? Of course. But for the most part, health and success go hand-in-hand. There IS a connection between the body, mind, and spirit.

So if you're really serious about success, work on staying fit. While there's a ton of things you can (and probably should) do to improve your physical condition, the following three – the "RED" areas – are great places to put your focus:

REST
Make sure you get enough sleep. There's no way you can be at your best if you start your workday already tired.

EXERCISE
Engage in some type of physical activity (working out, walking, playing a sport, etc.) several times a week.

DIET
Eat well-balanced meals. Minimize the "garbage foods" (you know what they are) and limit your portions.

Look your best

In order to be mahvelous, you must look mahvelous!

Fernando (Billy Crystal), Saturday Night Live

Ever notice that – with the exception of certain "show biz" types – most successful people just plain look good? If you haven't, pay closer attention and you'll see that it's generally true. High achievers care … about their careers and themselves. They care about the image they portray, which means caring about their appearance. To cite the somewhat worn but still valid cliché, they "dress for success." More accurately, they *groom* for success. And if you're serious about doing well and getting ahead, you need to as well.

The good news is that looking your best doesn't take big bucks or require that you dress like someone you're not. It's just a matter of taking pride in your appearance. It's about being neat and clean … about things like unwrinkled clothes, unscuffed shoes, moderate make-up and accessories, and good personal hygiene. And those are things that are applicable to (and important for) everyone – regardless of position, level, function, sex, race, or age.

Make an effort to look your best and you *will* feel better about yourself. And others (bosses, coworkers, customers) will respond more positively to you. It just works that way.

So, getting ready to leave for work? Look in the mirror. Do you see someone who doesn't care? Someone who apparently slept in his or her clothes? Someone trying to make a rock-star fashion statement? Or do you see a person who takes his or her job seriously and expects others to take him or her seriously as well?

Keep the boss informed

Fact: Nobody likes negative surprises.

Adage: If the boss don't know it, you ain't done it!

Those two pearls of wisdom provide all the rationale necessary for adopting yet another key to job and career success: Keeping the boss informed of what you're doing and what you're facing.

Oblivious managers tend to draw the wrath of employees. In order to be effective, managers need to know what's going on. (No huge revelation there!) They need to know about unexpected problems that surface so they can correct them; they need to know when employees experience obstacles to doing their jobs as expected; they need to know when their people perform well and go above and beyond the call of duty. But all those are difficult to do because of the ever-increasing spans of control that are a sign of the business times. Translated into simple terms: The trend continues to be fewer managers for the same (or larger) number of employees. There's no time to constantly be looking over employees' shoulders – and you'd hate that, anyway. So you need to help your boss (and yourself) out by providing periodic updates.

Experiencing an obstacle or unforeseen time delay on an assignment? Immediately inform your manager about the problem AND what you did/are doing about it. Worked late a couple of days this week to meet a deadline? Slip the boss a note. Making progress on a long-term project? Request a short meeting so you can update your manager. Not sure what the boss wants to know or how often he or she wants to be informed? ASK!

Successful people want and keep their managers "in the loop."

Act like an "owner"

There's no doubt that one of the very best ways to be successful at work is to act as if you own the place. But if you're thinking that means doing whatever you want, however you want, and whenever you want to do it, you need to think again. That's not what ownership is about at all. At least that's not what GOOD ownership is about.

So just what *is* it about? Well, imagine that you go into debt, big time, to start your own business. You rent space, lease equipment, buy supplies, hire people, hang "your shingle," and start working to attract customers. For you, everything is on the line. All of the decisions you make need to be carefully thought out ... all of the money (*your* money) that you spend must be done so wisely and as conservatively as possible ... each resource you have must be put to its very best use ... each customer must be treated like gold ... each product or service you offer must be dripping with quality ... each minute must be put to its most productive use. Fail to do so and you're out of business – you lose everything, and your employees lose their jobs. You are "The Big Kahuna" of stakeholders. And you most definitely will value and take care of the employees who look out for your interests and protect your investment. That's ownership! And those behaviors – plus many more like them – are your tickets to job success.

Starting right now, work on adopting the mind set that you're a huge stakeholder in the success of your organization. Fact is, you really *are* one. Act like it's your money, your equipment, your facility, your time, and your personal customers. You'll do well, go far, and easily outshine those who fail to follow this clear roadmap to a successful future.

Focus on "the big 2"

Looking for a crash course on business economics? Like to summarize the financial wisdom of the ages into simple, understandable terms? Look no further! Here are two strategies – "the big 2" – that demystify the subject and provide most of the guidance you'll need to make a positive name (and career) for yourself:

1. **Increase revenue** (make *more* of the green stuff).

2. **Decrease costs** (spend *less* of the green stuff).

Regardless of whether you're employed by a *for-profit* or a *non-profit* organization, both of these strategies are vital to "keeping the doors open" and keeping jobs (including yours) in place. And YOU can help make both happen – no matter your title, level, or function.

How can you help increase revenues? By providing superior service that makes customers want to buy more and come back again; by offering high quality goods and services that more people will want to purchase; by submitting ideas for new and innovative products; *and a whole lot more!*

How about reducing costs ... what can you do there? Maybe by researching cheaper vendors (or negotiating better prices with current suppliers); maybe by submitting cost-savings ideas; perhaps merely by avoiding waste or unnecessary use of sick time; *and a whole lot more!*

Take a piece of paper and jot down as many ways as you can think of to help your organization bring in more and shell out less. Get your boss's input. Then, start DOING them. And end each day by asking yourself: "What did I do today to increase revenue or decrease costs?"

Focus on "the big 2" and you'll not only be more successful, you'll also be eligible for an honorary degree in *simple* economics!

Perform with ethics and integrity

Keeping your job. Staying out of trouble (not to mention jail). Sleeping at night. Being proud of yourself. Earning the respect of others. Enhancing your career. If those things have little or no meaning to you, you'll probably do whatever you want at work – for as long as they'll let you get away with it (which, I'm guessing, won't be very long at all.) But if those benefits are as important to you as they should be, then it's critical that you behave ethically and perform with a high level of integrity.

Unless you've been stranded on a deserted island for the last several years, you know there are some serious problems out there in the business world. And it's absolutely imperative that you and your organization do *not* get caught up in them. The stakes are unbelievably high; the tolerance for inappropriate behavior, anywhere, is rapidly becoming ZERO; the need to ensure that people do "the right thing" is universal.

Sure, "ethics" is a huge and complex subject. But truth be told, the number one (and probably most important) key to always doing what's right is actually quite simple: **THINK before you act.** (What a novel idea!) That means checking decisions and planned activities to ensure "rightness" *before* implementing them.

Use the questions on the next page – or similar ones supplied by your organization – as your litmus test. Answering "no" or "I don't know" to one or more of these should be your clue(s) that: 1) You need a different approach, or 2) You probably need counsel and advice from your boss – or someone else in a position of authority.

THE ETHICAL ACTION TEST

A. Is it legal?

B. Does it comply with our rules and guidelines?

C. Is it in sync with our organizational values?

D. Will I be comfortable and guilt-free if I do it?

E. Does it match our stated commitments and guarantees?

F. Would I do it to my family or friends?

G. Would I be perfectly okay with someone doing it to me?

H. Would the most ethical person I know do it?

From: *Ethics4Everyone: The Handbook for Integrity-Based Business Practices*
The WALK THE TALK® Company
©Performance Systems Corporation

How Successful Am I? A Self-Assessment

Read each statement below. Think about it, and then respond as honestly as possible.

YES NO

Y N 1. I consistently work the hours I'm paid for and avoid using sick leave unless I'm really sick.

Y N 2. I take full responsibility for my actions, behaviors, and attitudes. I avoid "passing the buck" or blaming others for my problems and mistakes.

Y N 3. I know and follow ALL of the rules established by my organization.

Y N 4. When given a task or assignment, I regularly try to do MORE than is expected of me.

Y N 5. I make a habit of volunteering for work. When I see things that need to be done, I do them without waiting for others to take the lead.

Y N 6. I'm a considerate coworker. I regularly clean up after myself and avoid behaviors that may disturb others or cause them additional work.

Y N 7. I make a special effort to cooperate with the other members of my team and make sure that I consistently carry my share of the load.

Y N 8. I am committed to providing the best customer service possible. I continually place customer needs before my own.

Y N 9. I remember my promises and commitments, and I KEEP them.

Y N 10. I make a special effort to accept and support change rather than resist it. You can count on me to willingly try new things.

Y N 11. When I'm down, I avoid whining, complaining, or otherwise spreading negative feelings to my coworkers.

Y N 12. I look for (and seize) opportunities to help my coworkers be successful rather than just "being in it for myself."

Y N 13. I treat everyone with the same level of dignity and respect that I want for myself and the people I care about.

YES NO

Y N 14. I value and appreciate people with ideas, backgrounds, and demographic characteristics that are different from mine.

Y N 15. I continually look for (and create) opportunities to learn new things, and I avoid "I know all I need to know" thinking.

Y N 16. I make a habit of asking others (my boss, coworkers, and customers) for feedback on how I'm doing ... and I ACT on that feedback.

Y N 17. I make an effort to be patient with everyone I work with (and for) – cutting them the same "slack" that I wish for in return.

Y N 18. I truly appreciate the opportunities I receive, the people I work with, the customers I serve, and the fact that I *have* a job to be successful at.

Y N 19. Safety and health standards are critically important to me. I follow ALL of the guidelines and procedures existing to ensure a safe workplace.

Y N 20. I engage in specific behaviors (e.g., rest, exercise, diet) to keep myself in good physical health.

Y N 21. I maintain a neat, clean, and appropriate appearance at work.

Y N 22. I keep my boss informed of things I've done, what I'm working on, and any problems I'm experiencing that negatively impact my work.

Y N 23. I respect and protect my organization's equipment, resources, and facilities – just as if I owned the business and had my personal finances at stake.

Y N 24. I continually look for (and seize) opportunities to reduce costs and increase revenues (if appropriate) for my organization.

Y N 25. It's critically important for me to always perform with ethics and integrity ... and I do it!

Go back and highlight each of the statements for which you checked the NO box (there should be some ... unless, of course, you're perfect). These are the areas you should work on in order to increase your overall job success. Develop informal action plans, make a personal commitment to see them through, and get started. And for all those that you checked YES: Congratulations ... and keep doing what you're doing!

Closing Thoughts

Okay, so here you are at the end of the book. Hopefully you've read all the pages that preceded this one. And perhaps you've concluded: "Hey, there's nothing unique or special about this stuff ... no revelations ... no secrets revealed here." If that's your reaction, CONGRATULATIONS! You've broken the code! Succeeding at work is mostly a matter of common sense combined with healthy portions of commitment and self-discipline. Fact is, it's not all that hard to achieve job success – as long as you use your head and are willing to invest a little sweat equity.

The U.S. Army has a well-publicized recruiting slogan: *Be All You Can Be.* That phrase also happens to be the key to unlocking and enjoying a successful career. And for every person that thinks those words are lame or corny, there's someone else using and living by them in order to secure a great future ... someone who understands that a person IS what he or she DOES. Hopefully, *you're* that someone.

There's an all-too-common misconception floating around out there in the ranks of the employed. It's the belief that practicing the kind of behaviors found in this book is something you do for management. Well, nothing could be further from the truth. Yes, the organization does benefit when you do well. But YOU are the primary beneficiary of your own success. You are the person whose reputation is enhanced; you are the one whose opportunities and security will likely be increased; you are the one whose name is attached to everything you do.

Care about your organization.
But more importantly, care about yourself.

If a man is called to be a
street sweeper, he should sweep
streets even as Michelangelo painted,
        or Beethoven played music,
or Shakespeare wrote poetry.

    He should sweep streets so well
that all the hosts of heaven and earth
will pause to say, here lived a great
street sweeper who did his job well.

        ~ Martin Luther King, Jr.

Start Right...Stay Right
Individual Training/Orientation Resources

Start RIGHT...Stay RIGHT Self-Study Package!

With the *Start Right...Stay Right: Orientation Basics Self Study* materials you can affordably provide each one of your employees with a handbook and a personal use DVD* that effectively introduces them to 24 behaviors that will make them more successful on the job. With the Self Study package, each employee receives:

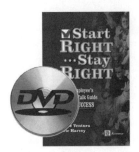

- ✓ *The Start Right...Stay Right Handbook*, a terrific introduction to the material that new hires can read quickly.
- ✓ *The Start Right...Stay Right: Orientation Basics Personal Use DVD* which builds off the information in the book by showing dramatic examples of the behaviors you want employees to either develop (or avoid).

Only $30.00 per program!
Visit **www.walkthetalk.com** for a free preview!

*The Personal Use DVD is licensed for a single user only and labeled accordingly. It cannot be used for group training. There is a minimum order of 30 units required for an initial order.

Start Right...Stay Right

Books in a Flash!™

28 pocket-sized reminder cards containing all the best ideas from *Start Right...Stay Right* in a handy bifold wallet.

Only $7.95 *each.*

Better yet, order the Start Right...Stay Right COMBO PAK *for only* $16.95!
(Includes the handbook and Mem-Cards)

Start Right...Stay Right
Group Training/Orientation Program

An easy-to-use training solution for communicating organizational expectations to all your employees.

What if you could easily show your employees the kinds of behaviors you expect from them, including everything from basic workplace etiquette (like being aware of personal hygiene & appearance) to showing appreciation to co-workers and taking initiative?

Start Right...Stay Right Orientation Basics will take viewers through a series of vignettes demonstrating the 24 success behaviors found in the *Start Right...Stay Right* handbook.

Here's the best part of this new video product: You can fully facilitate the training or just let the video stand alone. A Leader's Guide containing group exercises, activities and reproducible worksheets is included, but the video can also be used effectively without wrap-around discussion or activities.

The Start Right...Stay Right Group Training Program Includes:
- ✓ The 24 Demonstration Success Behaviors on VHS or DVD
- ✓ Leader's Guide
- ✓ PowerPoint *Presentation on CD-ROM*
- ✓ *10 copies of the* **Start Right...Stay Right** *employee handbook*

Only $649.00!

Visit www.walkthetalk.com for a free preview!

ORDER FORM
*Have questions? Need assistance? Call **1.888.822.9255***

✓ Check out the complete range of Start RIGHT ... Stay RIGHT products

QUANTITY	HANDBOOKS	MEM-CARDS™	COMBOPAKS
			(includes the book and MEM-CARDS™)
1-99	$9.95	$7.95	$16.95
100-499	$8.95	$6.95	$14.95
500+	*Please Call*	*Please Call*	*Please Call*

Start RIGHT ... Stay RIGHT Handbook	_____	copies X	_____	=$_____
Start RIGHT ... Individual Study Program*	_____	copies X	$30.00	=$_____
Start RIGHT ... Group Training Program	_____	copies X	$649.00	=$_____
Start RIGHT ... Stay RIGHT MEM-CARDS™	_____	paks X	_____	=$_____
Start RIGHT ... Stay RIGHT COMBOPAKS	_____	sets X	_____	=$_____

* Minimum order of 30 units required

Product Total	$_____
*Shipping & Handling	$_____
Subtotal	$_____
Sales Tax:	
Texas Sales Tax – 8.25%	$_____
CA Sales/Use Tax	$_____
Total (U.S. Dollars Only)	$_____

(Sales & Use Tax Collected on TX & CA Customers Only)

*Shipping and Handling Charges

No. of Items	1-4	5-9	10-24	25-49	50-99	100-199	200+
Total Shipping	$6.75	$10.95	$17.95	$26.95	$48.95	$84.95	$89.95 + $0.25/book

Call 972.243.8863 for quote if outside continental U.S. Orders are shipped ground delivery 7-10 days. Next and 2nd business day delivery available – call 888.822.9255.

Name_____ Title_____

Organization_____

Shipping Address_____

City_____ (No PO Boxes) State_____ Zip _____

Phone_____ Fax_____

E-Mail _____

Charge Your Order: ☐ MasterCard ☐ Visa ☐ American Express

Credit Card Number_____ Exp. Date_____

☐ Check Enclosed (Payable to The WALK THE TALK Company)

☐ Please Invoice (**Orders over $250 ONLY**) P.O. Number (required)_____

PHONE	FAX	MAIL
1.888.822.9255	**972-243-0815**	WALK THE TALK Co.
or 972.243.8863	**ON-LINE**	2925 LBJ Fwy., #201
M-F, 8:30-5:00 Cen.	**www.walkthetalk.com**	Dallas, TX 75234

Prices effective October 2005 are subject to change.